WHAT WOULD YOU DO?

FRIENDSHIP

JANA MOHR LONE AND SARAH JENNINGS

W

FRANKLIN WATTS

LONDON•SYDNEY

First published in Great Britain in 2024 by Hodder & Stoughton

Editor: Victoria Brooker
Design: Paul Cherrill
llustrator: Sarah Jennings
ISBN: 978 1 4451 8309 1 (hbk)
ISBN: 978 1 4451 8308 4 (pbk)
Printed in China

Franklin Watts
An imprint of Hachette Children's Group
Part of Hodder & Stoughton
Carmelite House
50 Victoria Embankment
London EC4Y 0DZ

An Hachette UK Company
www.hachette.co.uk
www.hachettechildrens.co.uk

Contents

Thinking about friendship

Our friends are important to us. *But what is a friend?*
How do you know if someone is *really* **a friend?**

Is it:

Having things in common?

Spending time together?

Having fun
when you're
with this person?

If someone cares about you and what you think and feel,
does that make them a friend? Is a friend someone who understands
and accepts you? Or is it someone you can trust with your secrets?

All of these might be true. And you might have different
friends for different reasons.

Friendships can be complicated, and sometimes even difficult.

You might have lots of questions about friendship.

Is someone still your friend even if you don't see them very often?

Do you have to like your friends all the time?

What do you do when you have a friend some of your other friends don't like?

These are all challenging questions, and often there is no single right answer. But there are many helpful ways to think about these kinds of issues.

How do you know if someone is a true friend?

Have you ever felt unsure about whether someone is a true friend?

Maybe you have a friend who always asks you if you want to hang out with them. But when you're with them, your friend doesn't seem that interested in you. You hear about what they think and what they've been doing, but they don't ask you anything about yourself.

Whenever you get together, you end up doing
what your friend wants to do.

What could you do?

You could say what you want or think.

Sometimes I feel you're not that interested in me.

I don't really want to play football. We did that last time. Can we ride bikes to the park?

You could tell your friend how you have been feeling.

Or you could think about whether you still want this friendship.

I don't think this friendship is working out.

What do you think?

If you say clearly what you want to do, maybe your friend will notice they haven't been paying enough attention to how you feel.

Letting your friend know how you're feeling can be scary. But perhaps they didn't realise their behaviour was upsetting you.

Or they might not change. If your friend doesn't seem to care about what you tell them, is your friend really a true friend?

Sometimes we have to work at our friendships. But if one friend is always controlling everything, maybe this isn't a true friendship. It might be time to consider developing friendships where there is more give-and-take.

What would you do?

Should your friends always come to your special events?

Have you ever had a good friend not come to your birthday party?

A good friend tells you she just feels like being alone and so won't be at your birthday party.

You feel hurt and disappointed that your friend won't be there.

What could you do?

You could tell your friend how you feel.

I know you want to be alone, but it's really important to me that you're there.

Or you could decide that it's okay for her not to come.

It won't be as much fun without her there, but I guess I should respect how she feels.

And you could think about if it's really important that your friend is at your party.

I suppose what matters is why she doesn't want to come. If she's feeling sad, I should understand.

What do you think?

It probably matters whether your friend has a good reason for not coming. If the reason is to stay home and watch TV, that might be harder to accept. If it's because your friend is having a hard time or is uncomfortable at the idea of being at the party, that would be different.

It also matters how good a friend this person is. The better the friend, the more disappointed you might be if they don't come to the party.

But the better a friend is, the more we try to understand their decision. Ask yourself if your desire to have your friend at the party is for your sake or your friend's sake.

Some people aren't comfortable at parties and your friend could have good reasons for not being there. But if a friend never comes to any events that are important to us, we are likely to question the friendship.

What would you do?

What if you have a friend your other friends don't like?

Some friends invite you to go to the cinema with them and you suggest inviting another friend of yours who is not part of this group but you know really wants to see the film.

You know that not everyone likes Taylor, but you do,
and you feel bad about not asking Taylor to come along.

What could you do?

You could go to the cinema with the group without Taylor.

Or you could tell your friends you're not going without Taylor and let them know how you're feeling.

I don't want to go without Taylor. I don't really understand why it's a big deal if he comes.

And you could think about whether you could do both.

Maybe I can go to the cinema with the group and then see it again with Taylor.

What do you think?

It probably affects how you feel if you think that your friends have a good reason for not wanting Taylor to come. Are they just being mean, or is Taylor not always an easy person to be around?

It also matters how much you want to go with the group. Will you regret it if you miss out and will that affect how you feel about Taylor? Or would you just as soon go with Taylor?

It's hard when a friend isn't liked by our other friends. Sometimes we understand why other people don't enjoy a friend's company, even though we do.

Other times we think a group is just being unkind and excluding someone without a good reason. That might lead us to question whether we really want to be part of this group.

We can also think about whether we can help our less popular friends.

What would you do?

When choosing teams, should you pick your friends first?

As team captain, you're in charge of picking your team's players. You know that it would make your friend Jordan happy to be chosen first, even though Jordan isn't very skilled at the game.

You want to make Jordan feel good, but you also feel a responsibility to choose the best team.

It doesn't feel fair to everyone else to choose one of the weakest players first.

The whole point of the game is to win, so shouldn't I pick the players who are best at the game?

Pick me!

What could you do?

You could decide that making Jordan happy is most important.

Or you could decide that being team captain means that you should choose players based on skill alone.

What do you think?

If you think it doesn't matter that much to Jordan, you'll be more comfortable choosing other players first. But if it matters a lot to Jordan, and Jordan is otherwise having a hard time, it might seem more important to choose Jordan early on.

It also matters how you see your role as team captain. It will make a difference if the game is just a bit of fun, or if it is part of a tournament.

It's not easy to balance your feelings for your friend and your role as team captain. You don't want to make your friend feel bad. But you also wonder if choosing team members based on friendship will affect the other players' feelings.

What would you do?

Is it okay to cancel plans if something better comes along?

You have planned to play video games and stay overnight at your friend Skyler's home this weekend, but another friend has just invited you to a concert of a band you love the same night.

You want to go to the concert, but you don't want to hurt Skyler's feelings.

What could you do?

You could tell Skyler that you have been invited to the concert and so have to change plans.

I've just been invited to a concert, so let's meet up next weekend instead.

Or you could decide that your original plan with Skyler should come first.

Skyler's been my friend for a long time. I shouldn't cancel just because there's something else I want to do.

You could also talk with Skyler about how you're feeling.

I know we have plans but it would be so great to go to this concert. Is that okay?

What do you think?

Most people believe it's not right to change plans any time a better offer comes along. But is it ever okay?

Think about whether your plans are especially important to Skyler right now for some reason? Does the band often give concerts in your town?

If you and Skyler spend time together frequently, that will affect how you feel. It will also matter if you have cancelled plans with Skyler in the past.

Think about how you would feel if your friend cancelled plans you had together. It would probably affect how you would react if the reason for the cancellation was a rare opportunity for your friend. But you might react differently if your friend often cancels.

When friends ask you to do something with them, maybe you should think about whether you are really free and happy to go before you say yes.

What would you do?

What can you do if you accidentally tell a secret?

A good friend tells you that he has a crush on someone in your class and asks you not to tell anyone. Later, you forget it's a secret and tell another friend. You realise you've broken your promise to your friend.

You are worried that if you tell your friend that you let the secret out, he won't want to be your friend anymore.

What could you do?

You could not say anything to your friend and hope he doesn't find out.

But if you don't tell him, you wonder if you will always be afraid he will eventually find out.

You could decide that he is likely to find out anyway, and that he will feel even more hurt if he hears it from someone other than you.

28

What do you think?

Obviously, it would hurt your friend to hear what you have done. So you might decide that telling them would make a bad situation worse.

But trust is a big part of friendship. In some ways, not telling your friend is a kind of double betrayal. If your friend hears what happened from you, it might feel like less of a betrayal.

It is possible that, even if you confess, your friend might not trust you again. Is it worth it to be honest? But how will you feel if you don't confess?

If it's likely that your friend will find out, that might lead you to want to confess. If it's not likely, you can decide whether it is better to be honest even if it leads to the friendship being damaged or ending, or whether less harm will come from keeping silent.

Ask yourself if your decision is based more on protecting yourself or on what will be best for your friend.

What would you do?

Notes for parents and teachers

Many of our most powerful childhood experiences involve friendship – finding new friends, sharing experiences with friends, being rejected by friends. We learn how to make and keep friends, ways to manage conflicts with friends – and that some friendships don't last.

Talk with your children and students about their friends. Do they have any favourite friends? Why do they like some children more than others? Are they having any issues with their friends?

Children often confront difficult ethical problems connected to their friendships. It's important that adults acknowledge that these issues – for example, whether it's okay not to choose a friend to be on your team, or what to do when you have a friend few other children like – can be complex and painful.

Ethical issues tend to involve deciding whether an action is the right choice and assessing the effects of our behaviour on other people as well as ourselves. Young people are confronted with these kinds of problems all the time.

What tools can we give children to help them develop their own conclusions about the ethical issues they face in their lives? Although in many circumstances it is necessary to tell a child, "This is wrong", it's also essential to help our children to learn how to analyse ethical problems themselves.

It is useful for children to be able to talk about their responses to the kinds of scenarios described in this book, and to learn strategies for evaluating the right thing to do in various circumstances. The goal is not necessarily to find that one right answer, but to be able to think through the issue and arrive at a reasoned decision.

Encouraging children to think about ethics is not about getting them to do what we think is right, but helping them to think for themselves about why certain things are right or wrong. Providing children with rules and guidance about ethical behaviour and good character is important, but many difficult dilemmas can't be resolved simply by applying a rule or principle.

Discussing with children their thoughts and ideas about ethical questions helps them to make better ethical decisions and to better understand the choices they do make. Ultimately, we want children to become reflective and sensitive, ethical adults. Thinking with them about topics, such as friendship, will help them get there!

Index